Table of Contents

W9-BMO-658

Introduction

Are you ready to learn Java programming? Java is a very powerful language that at the same time was made to be very easy to learn. There are many reasons why Java is so great. It is an absolutely FREE language. It is platform independent, which you will understand in a couple of minutes. Most importantly, Java is everywhere, on your phone, on your computer, and on many other devices that are around you every day.

The learning becomes complete only when we are able to apply what we have learned. In the case of programming, your learning becomes a success when you make an application out of your knowledge.

You might have used the calculator application available on your computer at least once. What about creating a calculator on your own? You are going to develop a cool calculator that will not only do basic mathematical calculations, but also ask you questions and interact with you based on your answers. So, you can use the calculator you design to help you in math and also to have some fun.

By the end of this tutorial, you will;

1. Understand how a Java program is processed.

2. Set up the basic Java development environment and start developing applications.

3. Learn how to set the PATH variable to make the program execution faster.

4. Understand what variables are and how to use them.

5. Learn to do math using Java.

6. Understand how to use conditional statements to decide the flow of execution.

7. Understand how to make your programs reusable and structured with the help of methods.

8. Learn how to collect inputs from the user.

9. Create a number of Java programs.

10. Develop a cool Talking Calculator.

It's alright if you don't understand all of what was said right away, that's what this book is about! So, let's get started...

Java Program Processing

In this section, I am going to explain to you simply how a Java program is processed. We said that Java is "platform independent." What does that mean? It means that the same Java program can run on many platforms, like Windows, OSx, and Linux, without changing even a single line of code, while other programming languages can only be used on certain platforms. For example C++ is run on the Xbox and Windows, primarily. The fact that Java can run on many platforms its power. How is it possible?

Before explaining the answer to the above question, let me ask you a few questions. Do you like pepperoni pizza? Do you ask your mother to prepare your favorite apple pie or cornbread? After having your delicious lunch or dinner, have you ever thought what was happening to that pizza, the pie, or the cornbread you ate?

In fact, we all have a very complex digestive system that turns the food we eat into nutrients that the body can easily absorb. Whether you eat a piece of apple pie or a piece of pizza, your digestive system digests the food by breaking it down into nutrients. Finally, our small intestine absorbs the nutrients so that you will have the energy to play outside, do sports, and play video games (even though you wouldn't think that takes up much energy.) Similar actions are happening in the case of Java as well.

The operating system of your computer might or might not be the same as that of your friend. You might be using a computer with Windows operating system, while your friend might be using a computer with Mac operating system.

Java code, also known as source code, that you write using your Windows computer or Mac computer gets converted to another language known as "ByteCode." Just like the food we eat, whether pepperoni pizza or apple pie, ByteCode turns into nutrients for the body to absorb.

The process of converting source code into ByteCode is known as "compilation." This is similar to the digestion process where food gets turned into nutrients. Regardless of the operating system upon which the source code exists, the ByteCode will be the same for the program no matter which operating system you run it on, just like the nutrients will be the same after digestion whether you eat apple pie, a double bacon cheeseburger, or drink milk.

The nutrients get absorbed into your body through the small intestine. Similarly, a virtual machine called "Java Virtual Machine" or "JVM" interprets the byte code to your computer so that your Java code is ready to work. The responsibility of JVM is translating the byte code into instructions that the underlying operating system understands.

See the image below that explains the processing of a Java program.

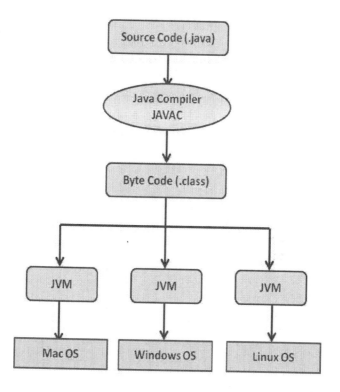

In this section, you have seen how the Java code is processed so that it can work on any computer without changing even a single line of code.

Setup the Environment

In this section, I am going to help you set up the environment that you need to write your Java code and also to check whether your code works correctly. You need to download and install a couple of software applications to set up the environment.

Java's environment is much like your room. It is set up a certain way, so that you feel at home, and so that you can work privately without distractions and other problems.

Similarly, Java also needs a proper environment to work in, which we are going to set up. Don't worry, I will explain to you how to do it step by step. Let's make the process simple and set up a basic development environment. Now you might be having doubts. Is there a complex development environment available then? Yes, I will tell you at the end of this tutorial how to setup the other environment. Until you become comfortable with Java coding, we will work on the basic or simple development environment.

As we proceed, you are going to download and install a few software applications. It is not at all a complex process. Still, if you are not comfortable with installing software applications, get help from someone who is. We need the following software programs to develop and run our Java applications:

1. A simple and powerful text editor to write our Java code.

2. Java Development Kit (JDK).

We are going to use "Notepad++." It is a free text editor that you can get from the Internet. You can think of Notepad++

as your notebook where you write your notes and keep them. Similarly, you can write your Java code using Notepad++ and save them. Now, if you do not have Notepad++ on your computer, then you can download Notepad++ application from the website at http://notepad-plus-plus.org/download/v6.6.9.html. Go ahead and install the program now.

The Java Development Kit provides the tools that we need to create ByteCode along with other tools, including Java Virtual Machine. You can think of Java Development Kit as your study room, with all facilities for your studying comfortably. The JDK consists of a number of items that help you develop your Java programs easily.

You can download JDK from the site http://www.oracle.com/technetwork/java/javase/downloads/jdk7-downloads-1880260.html. Visit this site and scroll down to get a screen like this:

Java SE Development Kit 8u20

You must accept the Oracle Binary Code License Agreement for Java SE to download this software.

◯ Accept License Agreement ● Decline License Agreement

Product / File Description	File Size	Download
Linux x86	135.24 MB	⬇ jdk-8u20-linux-i586.rpm
Linux x86	154.87 MB	⬇ jdk-8u20-linux-i586.tar.gz
Linux x64	135.6 MB	⬇ jdk-8u20-linux-x64.rpm
Linux x64	153.42 MB	⬇ jdk-8u20-linux-x64.tar.gz
Mac OS X x64	209.11 MB	⬇ jdk-8u20-macosx-x64.dmg
Solaris SPARC 64-bit (SVR4 package)	137.02 MB	⬇ jdk-8u20-solaris-sparcv9.tar.Z
Solaris SPARC 64-bit	97.09 MB	⬇ jdk-8u20-solaris-sparcv9.tar.gz
Solaris x64 (SVR4 package)	137.16 MB	⬇ jdk-8u20-solaris-x64.tar.Z
Solaris x64	94.22 MB	⬇ jdk-8u20-solaris-x64.tar.gz
Windows x86	161.08 MB	⬇ jdk-8u20-windows-i586.exe
Windows x64	173.08 MB	⬇ jdk-8u20-windows-x64.exe

You could see that a button "Decline License Agreement" is clicked on the screen. Click the other button "Accept License Agreement."

Java SE Development Kit 8u20

You must accept the Oracle Binary Code License Agreement for Java SE to download this software.

Thank you for accepting the Oracle Binary Code License Agreement for Java SE; you may now download this software.

Product / File Description	File Size	Download
Linux x86	135.24 MB	jdk-8u20-linux-i586.rpm
Linux x86	154.87 MB	jdk-8u20-linux-i586.tar.gz
Linux x64	135.6 MB	jdk-8u20-linux-x64.rpm
Linux x64	153.42 MB	jdk-8u20-linux-x64.tar.gz
Mac OS X x64	209.11 MB	jdk-8u20-macosx-x64.dmg
Solaris SPARC 64-bit (SVR4 package)	137.02 MB	jdk-8u20-solaris-sparcv9.tar.Z
Solaris SPARC 64-bit	97.09 MB	jdk-8u20-solaris-sparcv9.tar.gz
Solaris x64 (SVR4 package)	137.16 MB	jdk-8u20-solaris-x64.tar.Z
Solaris x64	94.22 MB	jdk-8u20-solaris-x64.tar.gz
Windows x86	161.08 MB	jdk-8u20-windows-i586.exe
Windows x64	173.08 MB	jdk-8u20-windows-x64.exe

You now need to download the file that is suitable for your operating system. If you are not sure the operating system on which your computer is running, whether Windows, Mac, Linux, or Solaris, get help from your parents.

If your operating system is Windows, you can download either of the last two downloads. The file Windows x64 is for 64 bit Windows operating system and Windows x86 is for 32 bit Windows operating system.

If you are not sure whether yours is 64 bit or 32 bit operating system, then

1. Right click the Computer or My Computer icon on your desktop.

2. Click the Properties option.

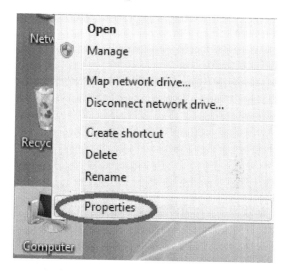

3. Check the System type information in the new screen. It will tell you whether your Windows operating system is 64 bit or 32 bit.

System

Manufacturer:	Toshiba
Rating:	**2.2** Windows Experience Index
Processor:	AMD E1-1200 APU with Radeon(tm) HD Graphics 1.40 GHz
Installed memory (RAM):	4.00 GB (3.59 GB usable)
System type:	64-bit Operating System
Pen and Touch:	No Pen or Touch Input is available for this Display

If you are using a Mac system, then download the file for Mac. In short, make sure that you download the correct file for your operating system.

Once the download is complete, install the file. The installation procedure will be different based on the operating system you are using, Windows, Linux or Mac, for example.

At some point during the installation process, you will be asked to specify the location where you want to install the Java Development Kit. In a Windows computer, it will be "C:\Program Files\Java" by default. Here, "C" is the name of the directory, and "Program Files" is the folder that will contain all your software applications. You can change the location if you want. However, make sure that you write down the path where you choose to install the JDK. Later we will need this information.

Once the installation is over, you are going to have the folder named Java (if you have not changed the name of the folder) at the location where you have installed the JDK. Don't worry even if you aren't able to recollect the new location that you specified. Take the piece of paper where you have written the details, and go to that folder.

Within that particular folder, you could find three subfolders named "jdk1.7.0_67," "jre6," and "jre7" if you have installed the JDK version 7. There could be slight differences in the names and number of folders if you have installed another version of JDK. However, there will be folders, at least one of which will be for the jdk and one for the jre.

We have already explained what JDK and Java Development Kit are. Now what is JRE? JRE or Java Runtime Environment is the runtime part of Java software, and it consists of the "Java Virtual Machine" or "JVM." Consider that our human body that contains not only our digestive system, but many other systems as well, including the neural system, the respiratory system, and nervous system, and others. Similarly, JRE contains parts that are required to run our Java program including Java Virtual Machine and some other.

Now we have installed the Java Development Kit required to develop and run our Java programs, but are we now ready to start coding? Not exactly. We have a couple more steps to go through in the next section.

Set the PATH variable

In this section, I am going to explain to you how to set a variable called PATH in order to execute or run your programs easily and quickly. You might know how to save a number into your phone so that you do not have to enter the phone number every time to call that person. You just need to click the name. Here, by setting a variable called "PATH," we need not have to specify a lengthy path every time while running our Java program. In other words, we will be able to run our Java programs easily and quickly if we set the PATH variable.

We have already seen that there will be at least one jdk and one jre folder in the main folder where you installed your Java Development Kit. If you do not remember where you installed your JDK, get it from the paper where you wrote it down. Now if you go to that particular folder and then open the jdk folder, you will find a folder name bin.

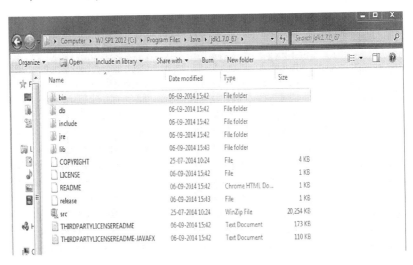

Could you find it? All our development tools are within this bin folder. As I have already mentioned, we have set up the basic development environment. So, we will be executing our Java applications from within a "command window." Do you know what a command window is?

Normally, how would you go to a folder in D:\ directory? You might click the My Computer icon on your desktop and then click the D:\ directory to reach the required folder. So, you are using graphical interface to reach the folder. You can also do the same thing without using the graphical interface also. You need the command window for this. Command prompt allows you to type computer commands and get the things done.

Normally, when you execute a program from the command window, you will have to specify the full path of the folder where all your tools reside. In our case, the path to the jdk folder needs to be specified every time. "Full path" is the full address of a file or folder. For example, if you have a file named "myFile.txt in D:\MyFirstFolder," the full path of myFile is "D:\MyFirstFolder\myFile.txt."

You can look at the paper where you wrote the location of the installation earlier and type in the full path, but chances are you could make a typo. Otherwise, you have to go to the particular folder and get the full path using Properties window. Isn't it difficult and time consuming? To avoid this, we are going to set an environment variable named "PATH." The PATH variable specifies a set of directories where executable programs are located. When we set the PATH, the operating system knows where to look for the tools that we need for Java development and execution.

The procedure to set up the PATH variable is different for different operating systems. Assuming that your operating system is Windows XP/2000/7, right click the My Computer or Computer icon on your desktop and click the option Properties. This will open a new window. There you will find an option "Advanced system settings" as in the following image (circled in red).

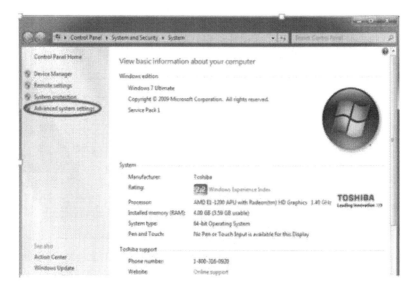

Click it, and you will get a new window. You could find a button named "Environment Variables" just above the OK and Cancel buttons. Click that button, and a new window will open. In the "System Variables" section (the second section on the window), look for "Path variable." Once you find it, click on it, and then click the Edit button shown below the System variables section (You will find New, Edit, and Delete buttons).

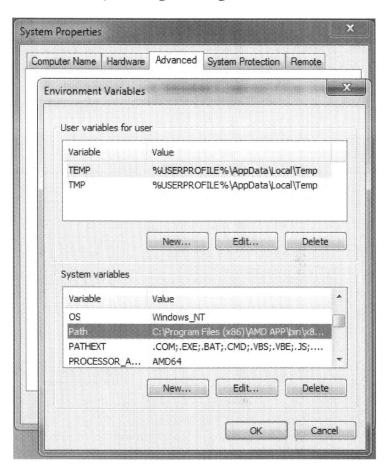

Now you will get a window like this:

We have to set the path value in the "Variable value" box. Make sure that you do not delete the value already existing in the Variable value box. When you store your friend's number on your mom's phone, do you delete a name and number that is already there? No, because that number could be your mom's friend's number. Similarly, the PATH already existing might be the path to some other executable files that you need to run some other applications. So, just add a semicolon at the end of the value in the box. That's to separate two paths.

Next, we need to get the path to our Java tools. We know all our development tools are now within the jdk/bin folder. You will have to go to the location where you installed your JDK to find this path. Get the details from the note you made. Once you get the path, copy it, and paste it after the semicolon. Click OK, and exit out of all the windows that you just opened up. Now the PATH variable is set.

In this section, we have seen how to set the PATH variable. I know you have gone through a very long process. Are you feeling tired or bored? Well now we're finally ready to go! The boring part is all over. Now we're ready to code.

First Java Program

In this section, I am going to teach you a simple Java program. This will help you understand how you will write Java code in Notepad++ and compile and run your program from the command prompt.

If you have already learned another programming language, the first program you probably tried was a "Hello World" program. If you are new to programming, a Hello World program is a simple program that displays the message "Hello World." This is normally used as the first program to demonstrate a programming language. Here, let's also start with a classic Hello World program. I am going to explain to you how to create a basic Java program with this example.

You have already installed the Notepad++ application, and you have the link to download and install Notepad++. Open the Notepad++ application. You will have its icon on the Desktop or in the All Programs list. When you open the application, a new 1 file will be opened automatically. Copy the following lines of code into that file.

```
// Our first Java program

public class HelloWorld

{

        // The entry point

        public static void main(String[] args)

        {

                // Display the message
```

System.out.println("Hello World!!!");

}

}

Do not worry about seeing these strange lines of code. It is very simple.

Every programming language has a set of rules referred to as "syntax." Syntax defines how the code should be presented so that the compiler can understand it and translate it into ByteCode in the case of Java. To make it simple, think of syntax as the grammar of English.

Computers are just machines that work based on instructions. If your instructions are wrong, the computer will not understand what it is expected to do. When you write Java code, make sure that your code syntax is correct. Otherwise, you will get errors when you try to run your application and will not get the expected result. If you already know C, C++, or PHP, you might find that the Java syntax is very similar to theirs.

In English, how do you find the end of a sentence? It is with a full stop (.). Every statement in the Java language ends with a semicolon (;) as at the end of the line "System.out.println("Hello World!!!");." A semicolon tells the program that it has finished one instruction.

Next, you could see three lines of code that start with // (two forward slashes). What are they? They are just comments that describe the code. In other words, they are just for the programmer to understand what he or she is telling the computer to do, but the computer completely ignores them. You might now be having a question in your mind, "Why should I waste time adding comments? I am developing the program and I know what the purpose of each line of code is." That is true when you do something for learning purposes or when you develop a very simple program like this HelloWorld program. However, do you really want to be a software developer or programmer? If so, you won't be developing simple applications with a few lines of code. You might be working in a team where you will develop a part of a software application, or you will be maintaining an application developed by others. Will you be able to understand other codes if they have not added proper comments, or will others be able to understand your code? No, because there are a thousand ways to solve one problem, and their way of solving it will likely be different from your way. You should get into the practice of adding comments whenever and wherever you can.

The first comment announces that this is our first Java program. If your comment is a single line comment, then you can add the comment just after two forward slashes. If you have a very lengthy comment that spans more than one line, you can enclose it within /* and */. There is no need to put two forward slashes at the start of each comment line if your comment is really lengthy.

Example:

//This is a single line comment.

/*This is a very lengthy comment.

I am doing a number of complex tasks.

So, I am adding comment like this. */

The multi-line comment also helps when you have a bunch of code that you don't want to run just yet, but also don't want to delete. You can just comment it out, and the computer will ignore it.

After the first comment, what do you see? A line of code: "public class HelloWorld." Are these new terms for you? I am going to introduce you to the term "class." What is a class? A class is a template or blueprint from which we can create objects. You can consider an object as a real world thing. A car is an object, an apple is another object, a bicycle is some other object.

Every object is built from a class. If you consider shape as a class, then triangle, square, rectangle and other shapes can be considered as objects of the type shape. If you consider vehicle as a class, then car, bus, and bicycle are some objects of vehicle class. A vehicle will have certain characteristics. These characteristics are the properties of the class. Some of the properties of a shape class could be number of sides, the area, and the perimeter. For now, just understand that each class can have a number of properties and methods.

You have learned a very important concept known as "object oriented programming." Object oriented programming is a kind of programming in which objects are used to create applications. As you proceed, you will find that everything in Java is based on classes and objects.

You now understand what a class is, but you might have noticed the term "public" just before the word "class." For the time being, just understand that the word "public" makes our class accessible to other classes. This will be explained in detail in the chapter <u>Methods</u>. This section is just to familiarize you with a simple Hello World program.

Every Java application must have at least one public class. You need to create a class with a special word or "keyword" class. In our program, the name of our class is HelloWorld.

We can later create objects of HelloWorld class if we want. When you save your file, you should make sure that the name of the file is the same as your class name.

After the second comment, you could find a line of code: "public static void main(String[] args)." Again, just understand that this is the main method of our program. This main method tells Java where the execution of this application should begin. The different terms including public, static, and void will be explained later in the <u>Methods</u> section.

The main method of any program should be in a public class. That is why we have included this main method in HelloWorld public class. The main method should be accessible to all other classes, and so we made it public like our HelloWorld class.

We are calling a function within the System library to display the string "Hello World!!!." The library is nothing but a collection of resources, just like a library of books that you have at your school or home.

Let's now try to run this code and see the result. You begin by creating a folder in any of your directories. You can create a folder just by right clicking inside the directory and going to New and then Folder options.

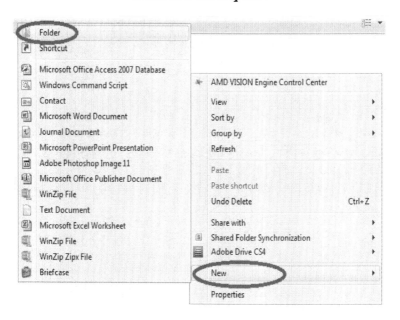

We are going to save all of our Java programs within this folder. This is just to keep all of our programs well organized and easily accessible. You can name your folder whatever you want. If you want to name it as "AwesomeJavaProjects", go ahead, because these java programs are going to be your awesome bragging rights. You can create it in C:\, D:\ or any directory you want. Go to the Notepad++ application, and click the File menu (on the top), and click Save option (circled in red).

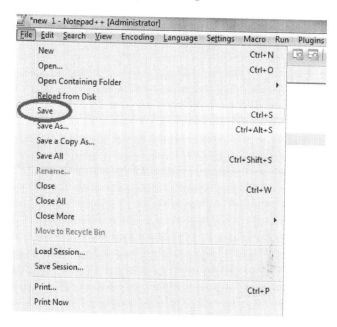

You will get a new window. Browse to the folder you have created just now to save all your Java programs. In the "File name" box, enter HelloWorld (make sure that you save it without any space between Hello and World). In the "Save as type" box, click the down arrow and select the option "Java source file (*.java)". Now your window will look like this:

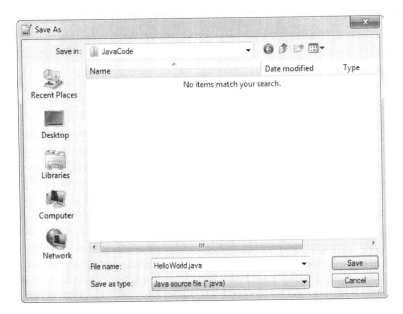

Click the Save button.

Open the command prompt. You do this by clicking the Windows icon on the bottom left corner of your screen and typing cmd in the box seen just above the Windows icon. Press the Enter button.

Go to the folder where you have stored your HelloWorld.java program using proper commands. If you are currently in C:\ directory, and your folder is in D:\ directory, you will have to enter D: in the command prompt.

Now using cd command, reach your folder.

If your folder is not directly within the C: or D: directory, you might have to enter cd command followed by the folder name multiple times. For example, if you have stored your java file within the folder D:\MyCode\AwesomeJavaProjects, then you will have to enter "cd MyCode" first and then enter "cd AwesomeJavaProjects" next.

If you don't want to keep switching back and forth between the windows explorer and command prompt to see what is in each file, then just type "dir" (without the quotes) and press enter. You will see a list of everything in the folder that you are in. If something has <DIR> before its name, then that means it is another folder that you can go into.

Once you reach your program folder, type "javac HelloWorld.java" and press the Enter key. If you go to the folder where you saved the java file, you will find a new file named HelloWorld.class.

What magic is this? Did you go into your folder and create a file named HelloWorld.class? No, it is done by the Java compiler. The Java compiler compiles our source code into ByteCode and HelloWorld.class is the ByteCode file.

Next, come back to the command prompt, and type "java HelloWorld" (without a "c" at the end of java this time). You do not need to type "HelloWorld.java" or "HelloWorld.class." Now if everything is right, you will see the output "Hello World!!!" on the command prompt like this:

Yes!!! You have created your first Java program!

Do you remember the long procedure we went through to set the PATH variable? Suppose we had not done it, that is we had not set the PATH variable. Then, just before compiling the program (before "javac HelloWorld.java"), we would need to have added a line "set path=%path%; C:\Program Files\Java\jdk1.7.0_67\bin". Each time we execute a new program, we would have had to add this line. It is really good that we set the PATH variable though it was slightly complex, isn't it?

After going through a very lengthy procedure, you learned a number of concepts including the most important concept of object oriented programming. Not only that, you also developed your first Hello World program in Java and executed it successfully. Congrats to you! You have started on your path to becoming a programmer!

Compare Real Life Scenario and Programming Scenario

Programming is nothing but getting help from computers and some programming languages to perform things that would have been difficult if we did it on our own. Just think of doing some complex mathematic calculation. For example, you want to multiply 74898 by 39765. How long will it take you to get the answer? It might take at least two or three minutes unless you are a mathematical genius. However, let me tell you, if the computer is doing the same calculation, you will get the answer in a blink of an eye. Shall we try?

What do you need to do, to do the above mathematic calculation on your own? Of course, you need a piece of paper and a pen or pencil. Then, you need to write the two numbers to be multiplied. You also have to do some mental math and write the answer. In the case of programming, we need some place to store the numbers to be multiplied and also the result. We need Java math techniques to perform calculations and something more to complete our calculator. I am going to explain this to you step by step so that you can apply each of these techniques when you actually program. Now let's start.

Variables

When we develop a calculator, we need to store two numbers and the answer somewhere in the memory of the computer. I told you at the beginning that we are going to develop an interactive talking calculator. This calculator will do some math for you. That is, if you provide two numbers to the calculator, it will add, subtract, multiply, or divide after asking you what you want to do with those two numbers.

In addition to that, this talking calculator is also ready to interact with you. It will ask you some interesting questions and will respond to you based on your answers. We now need to store not only numbers, but also some text values. How are we going to do it? Here, "variables" come into picture. A variable is nothing but a memory space to store values. We call that value to be used using the variable's name that we assign to it.

You can store different types of data in a variable. In the following picture, you could find that different types of data such as text, number, decimal number, character, and true/false values are stored in different locations. These data types can be classified into two groups, "primitive data types" and "reference/object data types."

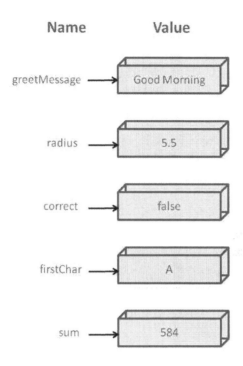

Name   **Value**

greetMessage ⟶ Good Morning

radius ⟶ 5.5

correct ⟶ false

firstChar ⟶ A

sum ⟶ 584

Primitive Data Types

There are a number of built-in (readily available) or primitive data types in Java. They are "integers," (byte, short, int, and long), "decimals" (float and double), "Boolean," and "char." You can store an integer using any of the first four data types and a decimal value using either of the next two data types.

- Integer value is a positive or negative number without any decimal place. There are four types of integer values including "byte," "short," "int," and "long."

  - A byte is the basic unit of memory made up of 8 bits that can store values from -128 (2^7) to 127 (2^7-1) both inclusive.

33

- A short can store values from -32,768 (2^{15}) to 32,767 (2^{15}-1).

- The int is one of the most commonly used data types in Java. It can store values from -2,147,483,648 (2^{31}) to 2,147,483,648 (2^{31}-1).

- You can use long-type variables if you want to store really large values.

Examples:

byte byteVal = 67;

short shortVal = -650;

int intVal = 200000;

long longVal = 6778005876543;

- A decimal value is referred to as a floating point in programming. A floating point is a positive or negative number with a decimal place. There are two types of floating point values including float and double.

  - A float is made up of 32 bits.

  - A double is made up of 64 bits.

Examples:

> *float decVal1 = 23.4;*

> *double decVal2 = 88.4;*

- There are two more primitive data types in Java: boolean and char.

  o The boolean data type is to store true or false values.

  o Things like single letters and other keyboard symbols go into the char type, but you can only have one letter or symbol in a char variable. Also pay attention to the single quotes used for chars. Strings, which I will show you in a second, use double quotes instead.

Examples:

> *char firstChar = 'A';*

> *boolean flag = true;*

Reference or Object Data Types

In addition to primitive data types, there are "reference" or "object data types" as well.

- The string is a most commonly used object data type that stores text values. When you create a variable of type String, you should specify it as String (with a capital "S").

Example:

String name = "John Smith";

Note the double quotes used here, unlike the single quotes used for char.

Are you ready to develop a simple program to understand the concept of variables clearly? This application will welcome a user named John Smith and tell him his age.

Open the Notepad++ application, and copy the following lines of code into a new file.

```
// Program that illustrates Variables concept

public class VariableExample

{
        // The entry point

        public static void main(String[] args)

        {
                // declare an integer variable

                int age = 29;

                // declare two string variables

                String firstName = "John";
```

```
String lastName = "Smith";

// Display the message

System.out.println("Welcome " + firstName
+ " " + lastName + "!!! You are " + age + " years old.");

        }

    }
```

Let's recap. How will you name this file when saving? Can you name it the way you want? No, never. The name of the file should match the class name. When you store the number of your friend Hannah on your phone, will you save it as Helen? No, similarly the name of the class should be the same as the name of your file.

Hence, the file should be saved as VariableExample. Do not forget to save it as a java source file (.java). Open command prompt and go to the folder you store all your Java examples. Enter javac VariableExample.java and then java VariableExample. If everything is done correctly, you will get an output like this:

In this program, we have declared an integer variable named "age" to store the age value (*int age = 29;*) and two string variables named firstName and lastName to store first name and last name respectively (*String firstName = "John"; String lastName = "Smith";*). Finally we displayed a message. Have you noticed I used + to join the strings? Why did I put a space after the Welcome value before the closing double quotes? Otherwise, the start of the message would have been "WelcomeJohn" without a space between Welcome and John.

Again, I want to display the first name and last name separated by a space. That is why, I have added a space " " between firstName and secondName. Now if you go through the whole message, you can identify where I have added spaces to make the message neat and clean. Change the values of age, first name, and last name with your age, first name, and last name. Run the program. Be happy to see your name and age as the output!!!

What is a "strongly typed language"?

Now I am going to explain a new concept to you. Have you ever heard that Java is a "strongly typed language?" What does it mean? Hey, don't panic! It is a very simple concept.

When someone tells you "Ann is the sister of Alan," you understand that;

> **a)** Ann is a girl or woman because we use the term sister to refer to a girl or woman.

> **b)** Ann has at least one sibling, because to be a sister, you need to have at least one sister or brother, also known as a sibling.

Henceforth whenever you hear about Ann, you will think of her as a girl having a sibling. She will not be included in other categories like "boy," "husband," or even "only child."

Similarly, strongly typed language means that once you define a variable of a particular data type, you cannot use it to store another data type. For example, you define a variable named "firstNum" of int type, then you are allowed to store only integers within firstNum, not String or Boolean.

In fact, there are some other programming languages that do not need you to classify the type of variable when you create it. In other words, some programming languages allow you to store different types of data in the same variable, but not simultaneously, of course. Such languages are known as "loosely typed languages." Some of the loosely typed languages are "Perl" and "JavaScript." Once you understand the basic Java concepts, learning JavaScript is an easy task.

Try the following code to understand this concept. In this program, we declare a variable of type integer and then try to use the same variable to store text value.

```
// Program that illustrates strongly typed

public class StrongType
{
    // The entry point
    public static void main(String[] args)
    {
        // declare an integer variable
        int myVal = 29;
        // display the value
        System.out.println("The integer value is " + myVal);

        // try to store a string value in the myVal variable
        myVal = "My Value";
        System.out.println("The modified value is " + myVal);
    }
}
```

I know you're smart, so I don't want to go over how to save the file, compile, run it on command prompt, and see the output. Only one thing, the name of the file should be same as the class name.

Did you get the output? Do not be worried when you get an error after compilation (javac StrongType.java). It is because that we tried to save a String value "My Value" in the variable myVal which we have already declared of type int. Try changing the value to 300 instead of "My Value." That is the statement myVal = "My Value;" should be changed to myVal = 300; . Save the file, and compile and run it from command prompt. I know you have the correct output now. Good? Good.

One more thing you should know about variables is that they have a defined lifespan referred to as "scope." The scope is determined by where a variable is declared. Curly braces {} define the scope of any variable. In other words, variables created after an opening curly brace normally have scope until the corresponding closing curly brace.

Try the following code on your own. In this program, we will try to access a variable from a location where it does not have scope. Let's see what happen.

```java
// Program that illustrates variable scope

public class VariableScope

{

        // The entry point

        public static void main(String[] args)
```

```
{

    {

    //declare two integer variables

    int firstNum = 15;

    int secondNum = 25;

    //calculates the sum

    int sum = firstNum + secondNum;

    //displays the sum

    System.out.println("The sum is " + sum);

    }

    //calculates the product

    int product = firstNum * secondNum;

    //displays the product

    System.out.println("The product is " +
product);

    }

}
```

It is obvious that you will get an error after compilation.

Why? The reason is that you are trying to access two variables, firstNum and secondNum, at a place where it does not have scope. Those variables have scope only until the sum is displayed. After that, those two variables are destroyed. If you see the detail of the error, you could find that the compiler cannot find symbols firstNum and secondNum.

If you want to get the correct output, remove the opening curly brace just above the comment //declare two integer variables and also the closing curly brace before the comment //calculates the product. Now try, and you will get the output for sure.

In this section, we discussed what variables are, different types of variables, and the scope of a variable. We have also seen why Java is called a strongly typed language.

Java Math and Operators

In this section, I am going to explain to you how to do math operations using Java. It is as simple as the math you learn in school. Our calculator has two parts, mathematic calculations and simple interaction.

To perform mathematic calculations, we use the operators +,- ,/,x, and =. We also use these symbols in Java. As in mathematics, an operator is a symbol that represents an operation, and there should be at least one operand to perform an operation.

The operators +, -, *, /, %, ++ and -- are known as "arithmetic operators."

- + is for addition
- - is for subtraction
- is for multiplication
- / is for division
- % is to get the remainder after division
- ++ is to increase the value by 1. ++ is called increment operator.
- -- is to decrease the value by 1. -- is called decrement operator.

The following application performs some basic mathematical calculations using arithmetic operators. You will add two numbers, subtract one number from another number, multiply two numbers, divide one number by another to calculate the quotient and the remainder, add 1 to a number and finally subtract 1 from a number.

```
// Program that performs mathematical calculations
public class MathCalculations
{
        // The entry point
        public static void main(String[] args)
        {
                // declare two integer variables
                int firstNum = 35;
                int secondNum = 27;
                // addition
                int sum = firstNum + secondNum;
                // subtraction
                int difference = firstNum - secondNum;
                // multiplication
                int product = firstNum * secondNum;
                // division
                int quotient = firstNum / secondNum;
                // remainder
                int remainder = firstNum % secondNum;
```

// displays the results

```
System.out.println("The sum of " + firstNum + " and " + secondNum + " is " + sum + ".");

System.out.println("You will get " + difference + " if you subtract " + secondNum + " from " + firstNum + ".");

System.out.println("The product of " + firstNum + " and " + secondNum + " is " + product + ".");

DecimalFormat df = new DecimalFormat("###.##");

System.out.println("The quotient of " + firstNum + " / " + secondNum + " is " + quotient);

System.out.println("The remainder of " + firstNum + " / " + secondNum + " is " + remainder);

System.out.println("Add 1 to " + firstNum + " (increment) to get " + (++firstNum) + ".");

System.out.println("Subtract 1 from " + secondNum + " (decrement) to get " + (--secondNum) + ".");}

}
```

You will get the correct output for sum, difference, product, quotient, remainder, increase by one, and decrease by one. You will use the arithmetic operators +, -, *, /, %, ++ and -- respectively to do this. I am sure you know how to add two numbers, subtract one number from another, multiply two numbers, add 1 to a number, and subtract 1 from a number. It is easy for you. Isn't it? However, do you have any doubts when it comes to division? How will you divide 35 by 27? Take a piece of paper and a pen. Divide 35 by 27. Hey, don't check the answer now. Once you complete, check whether both of us have got the same answer. OK?

Here is my answer.

			0	1
2	7	3	5	
		0		
		3	5	
		2	7	
			8	

Here 35 is the dividend, 27 is the divisor, 1 is quotient and 8 is the divisor. Didn't you get the same values for quotient and divisor when you run your program?

In addition to arithmetic operators, there are some more types of operators in Java.

One group is "relational operators" that are used to compare two values. The relational operators include

- < (less than)

- > (greater than)

- != (not equal to)

- == (equal to)

- <= (less than or equal to)

- >= (greater than or equal to)

There are also "logical operators" which are mainly used to check conditions. We will see how to check conditions in the following section.

Logical operators include

- && (AND)

- || (OR)

- ! (NOT)

There are also operators such as "assignment operators," "bitwise operators," and some "miscellaneous operators." However, we will not be using any of these operators in our project. Moreover, you will be using arithmetic operators, relational operators, and logical operators most often even in the future when you create more complex programs. We are also going to use some of these operators as we proceed.

In this section, we have seen different types of operators. We need arithmetic operators mainly for the creation of our talking calculator, so here we have discussed arithmetic operators in detail.

Conditional Statements

In this section, I am going to explain how to decide the flow of execution in Java using "conditional statements." The calculator we are planning to develop needs to perform different calculations. For example, if the user wants to add two numbers, it should add. If the user wants to multiply two numbers, it should do so. If the user does not want to perform any mathematical calculations, but just interact with the calculator and have fun, then that also should be possible. We need to perform different things based on different conditions. Conditional statements can help us here.

Your teacher has probably told your class this before: "If you didn't turn in the assignment, then you'll get a zero, but if you did, then you're fine." Let me just arrange the same sentence in a different way.

If (you didn't turn in the assignment)

Then you'll get a zero

But if you did   Then you're fine

I did not change your teacher's statement at all. Did I? I just included the section "you didn't turn in the assignment" within parentheses. Correct? Now what is that within the parentheses? It is the condition which will be either satisfied or not satisfied. If that condition is satisfied, the first thing will happen. Otherwise, the second thing will happen, not the first one. Is it clear? We are using similar syntax for checking conditions in Java with a few changes.

The syntax of a conditional statement is as follows:

if (condition1)

{

      statements that are to be executed if condition1 is satisfied

}

else

{

      statements that are to be executed if condition1 is not satisfied

}

Here the condition1 will return either true or false. Let's try an example as always. This program will compare two numbers and display a message telling us whether the two numbers are same or not.

```
//Example that illustrates simple if--else

public class Conditions

{
    //The entry point

    public static void main(String[] args)
```

```
{
        // declare two integer variables

        int firstNum = 17;

        int secondNum = 17;

        // Checking for the condition whether first number
and second number are the same

        if(firstNum == secondNum)

        {
                // statement to be executed if the condition is
satisfied

                System.out.println("The first number " +
firstNum + " is equal to the second number " + secondNum);

        }
        // otherwise

        else

        {
                // statement to be executed if the condition is
not satisfied

                System.out.println("The first number " +
firstNum + " is not equal to the second number " + secondNum);

        }

}
```

}

Have you noticed the == between firstNum and secondNum? It is a relational operator, which we have discussed earlier. Have you compiled and run the program? Did you get the output? Good. Try changing the firstNum and secondNum values, and see the difference in the output.

Now is the conditional checking always as simple as this? No, sometimes there could be more than two conditions to be checked. Has your teacher ever told you "If you didn't turn in the assignment, you'll get a zero, if you did, you're fine, and if you think you turned it in, but received a zero, then come talk to me."

Now going back to our Java learning, we have the syntax ready to handle this kind of situation. That is to check for more than two conditions. The syntax is as follows:

if (condition1)

{

        statements that are to be executed if condition1 is satisfied

}

else if(condition2)

{

        statements that are to be executed if condition2 is satisfied and condition1 is not satisfied

}

```
else if(condition3)

{

        statements that are to be executed if condition3 is
satisfied and condition1 and condition2 are not satisfied

}

else

{

        statements that are to be executed if none of the above
conditions are true

}
```

These conditions will be checked in the same order they are given. You can have as many "else" if conditions as you want. The program will reach the final else section only if none of the above specified conditions are satisfied.

Let's modify the above example to understand the if...else if...else conditional statement clearly. This program will compare two numbers and tell us which number is greater, which number is smaller, or whether both the numbers are equal. Try this code.

```
//Example that illustrates if--else if---else

public class Conditions

{

    //The entry point
```

```
public static void main(String[] args)

{

        // declare two integer variables

        int firstNum = 87;

        int secondNum = 67;

        // Checking for the condition whether first number is
less than second number

        if(firstNum < secondNum)

        {

                // statement to be executed if the first
condition is satisfied

                System.out.println("The first number " +
firstNum + " is less than the second number " + secondNum);

        }

        // Checking for the condition whether first number is
greater than second number

        else if(firstNum > secondNum)

        {

                // statement to be executed if the second
condition is satisfied

                System.out.println("The first number " +
firstNum + " is greater than the second number " + secondNum);
```

```
        }

        //otherwise

        else

        {

                //statement to be executed if both the above
conditions are not satisfied

                System.out.println("The first number " +
firstNum + " is equal to the second number " + secondNum);

        }

      }

    }
```

Compile and run the code. Check whether the output is logically correct. If you get a message, "The first number 87 is less than the second number 67," then, you have to go back and see what you did wrong. One thing to check would be to make sure that the > or < signs are in the right places. "Remember the computer does *exactly* what it is told, so most of the time you just simply typed something wrong. Always make sure that the output you get is logically correct.

When you begin to learn programming, you might feel very happy when you get no errors after compilation. It just means that your syntax is correct. However, it does not ensure that your output is correct because compilers could not find logical errors in your code. So be very careful, OK? Now try changing the firstNum and secondNum values, and see the difference in the output.

In this section, we have learned how we can decide the flow of execution based on different conditions. We had a look at simple if---else statements and complex if---else if---else statements.

Methods

In this section, I am going to explain the concept of "methods." Methods make your code reusable and organized. We will see how to create a method and also "invoke" it. In programming, invoke is the correct term to refer to calling or using a method.

What do we call a method in our day to day life? You might have your own secret methods of study, or your own method of beating a game. Your secret method of study could be taking short notes that help you remember the whole concept easily, or your method of beating the game could be to stay sneaky until the time is right to take down your opponent. Anyway, a method is made of multiple steps that we follow to accomplish something.

In the world of programming, a method is very much similar to our real world method. A method is nothing but a few lines of code that contain a series of statements to accomplish something. You have developed a secret method of study or of gaming, but would it be useful if you didn't try it out? No, it wouldn't. Similarly, just creating a method will not execute the statements inside that method. We need to invoke or call the method to get the statements executed.

The applications that we develop using any programming language are not as simple as the above ones we have already created. We need to perform lot of complex things. Just think of our calculator itself. Do you think that we can develop the program with 20 or 30 lines of code? No, we will have to write hundreds of lines of code. I don't say this to scare you, because it will all make sense to you, and you'll find that it doesn't take too long. As you have already seen, a line of code is much shorter than a line in a book.

I will now tell you why and when we need methods. Methods make our program more readable, structured, and reusable. When we divide a complex program into smaller, logical blocks of code, the program becomes more readable and structured. Again, we do not have to write the same lines of code again and again to do the same task repeatedly. Write it once, and call it as many times as you need. Methods also make the development and testing easier as the tasks are logically grouped.

See the syntax of a Java method:

visibility static/instance returnType methodName (parameter1, parameter2, …)

    {

        lines of code

    }

An example:

public static int calculateSum(int first,int second)

    {

        int sum = first + second;

        return sum;

    }

Are you ready to create and invoke a method? Before that, let me make you comfortable with the terms like "public," and "static." Have you seen these words before? Yes, you saw these words back in our first Hello World program. Am I correct? I have promised you that I will explain those terms in the Methods chapter. This is the Methods chapter that I have been referring to. Now it is time to understand what those jargons are. Read carefully.

Any method should have a "method header" and a "method body." The method body contains the lines of code that do a particular job. The method header gives the basic information about your method to Java. In our example, *public static int calculateSum(int first,int second)* is the method header.

Let's see all the items in the method header one by one. You see public is the first value in the method header. What is it? It is known as an "access modifier."

Before explaining the topic, let me ask you a simple question. Suppose your father has an expensive car. Will everyone, including your relatives, neighbors, or your father's colleagues be allowed to drive that car? No, your father or your mother might be the only people who drive that car. Am I right? Now suppose your father has a cheap used car that he plans to sell very soon. Your father might allow even his colleagues or neighbors if they ask him to use it. Here, your father decides who can access a thing (expensive and cheap cars here) based on some criteria.

Similarly in Java, access modifiers decide whether other classes can use a class or the members of a class. What are the members of a class? The members of a class are "properties" and "methods."

There are mainly four types of access modifiers. They are;

1. Private
2. Public
3. Default
4. Protected

There are some items which are used or accessed only within a private group (like the expensive car used only by your own family members) and those items are referred to as "private." On the other hand, there are certain items which are accessed not only within a class, but also from outside (like the cheap used car) and those items are referred to as "public."

If you do not specify any modifier before a class, property, or method, it is considered as a "default modifier" and such items are accessed only within a specific "package." A package is a collection of classes. Just think of a package as a collection of books at your home or school. A protected class, property, or method is accessible to a class and its subclasses. These concepts are a bit advanced, and you need not know at this point of time. So, do not worry even if you could not understand default and protected access modifiers completely.

After the word public, the next one is "static." This value specifies whether your method is static or "instance." A static method can be called without creating an object of the class. Don't you remember the main method of our class? It's public static void main. We have not created any object for our class to access that method.

Suppose your method is an instance method. Then you will have to create an object of the class to access that particular method. How will you create an object of a class? It is very simple. Suppose you have a class named Shape and you want to create an object named triangle.

Shape myTriangle = new Shape();

This statement creates an object named myTriangle of the class Shape.

Suppose the class has an instance method named calculateArea, and you want to calculate the area of the triangle. Then, we will invoke the method like

myTriangle.calculateArea();

Suppose the method is static. You could invoke the method just by the following statement (no object is required).

calculateArea();

That is the difference between static methods and instance methods. You have to specify the keyword static to make a method static, but you do not have to specify any keyword if your method is instance. That is, a static method declaration could look like this:

public static void calculateArea();

whereas an instance method declaration could look like this:

public void calculateArea();

Some methods, after the execution, return a value, and its type should be included in the method header. If the method does not return any value, you should specify it as void. Do you remember our main method in all our Java programs? We used to specify the return value of our main method as void (public static void main) because the main method does not return any value.

Next is the method name. Try to give a meaningful name to your method. How awkward would it be to name a method that adds two numbers as myInput or myValue? Have you heard that your handwriting reflects your personality? Being a software professional, I would say that the code you write reflects your personality too. Always make it neat, readable, structured, and organized.

Again coming back, some methods will require inputs to execute. Just think of our calculator. Suppose we create a method named calculateSum to add two numbers. Of course, the numbers will be entered by the user. The method needs those two numbers to calculate the sum. These inputs we pass to our method are called "parameters." You should specify the parameters along with their data types (int firstNum or double product) just after the method name. You should enclose the parameters within brackets. You should separate parameters with commas (if more than one).

Try the program given below. This program uses a method called calculateSum to find the sum of two numbers.

```
//Example that illustrates use of methods

public class FirstMethod

{

    //The entry point

    public static void main(String[] args)
```

```
    {

        // declare two integer variables

        int firstNum = 87;

        int secondNum = 68;

        // invoking the method

        System.out.println("The result is " +
calculateSum(firstNum,secondNum));

    }

    // creating the method.

    static int calculateSum(int first,int second)

    {

        int sum = first + second;

        return sum;

    }

}
```

You could find that we have not specified the access modifier for the calculateSum method, so it has the default access modifier. Also, the method is declared as static, and you are not creating any object of the class FirstMethod. Again, as the method returns an integer, the sum of two integers, and hence we specified the return type as int in the method header. We passed two parameters first and second along with their data type (int) to calculate the sum.

Try changing the method to instance type by just deleting the static keyword in the calculateSum method header. Are you getting an error like this after compiling the application?

```
Administrator: C:\Windows\system32\cmd.exe
Microsoft Windows [Version 6.1.7601]
Copyright (c) 2009 Microsoft Corporation. All rights reserved.

C:\Users\user>D:

D:\>cd JavaCode

D:\JavaCode>javac FirstMethod.java
FirstMethod.java:11: error: non-static method calculateSum(int,int) cannot be re
ferenced from a static context
        System.out.println("The result is " + calculateSum(firstNum,secondNum));
                                               ^
1 error

D:\JavaCode>
```

The error message clearly states the error. Our method is a non-static (instance) method, and we are trying to access it without creating an object. So, add the following line of code just before the comment //invoking the method.

//Creating an object of the class

FirstMethod callMethod = new FirstMethod();

Invoke the method like this:

> *callMethod.calculateSum(firstNum,secondNum);*

instead of

> *calculateSum(firstNum,secondNum);*

Now you got the output. Right? When you read error messages, pay attention to the first error message that pops up, the one at the top of the list of errors, because this is almost always the error that needs to be fixed. All of the other errors are simply there because your first error broke multiple things at once.

In this section, we have seen how to create and invoke a method. We also found out the different values to be added in the method header.

Scanner Object

In this section, we will see how to collect the values entered by the user, and then use those values to make our calculator more interesting and useful.

In all of our previous samples, we set values to our variables inside the program itself like int firstNum = 87 or int age = 29. We never asked anything from the outside world. Would you like it if your father did not ask about your interests and made you take a class that you never wanted to study? No. Similarly, if you want to satisfy your users, you should ask the needs and interests of the user.

If you are creating an interactive program, you will have to collect inputs from the user and process those inputs. Even in our calculator, we should accept two numbers from the user to perform mathematical calculations. How will we do it? Java provides a class named "Scanner" with a large number of methods to collect inputs from the user. This Scanner class is available within a package named "util."

Are you using any toy or electronic device imported from China or some other country? "Import" means to bring something from a different place or context. In programming, import has the same meaning. If we want to use the Scanner class within our program, we should bring it in using the keyword *import*, like this:

import java.util.Scanner;

Now we need to create an object of the class Scanner. We have already seen how to do it.

Scanner input = new Scanner();

We are going to get input from the keyboard, right? So, we should have something to connect to the keyboard, and it is done using "System.in." System.in is an input stream. In other words, it takes input from the outside world. You need to pass System.in as the parameter while creating an object of Scanner class.

Scanner input = new Scanner(System.in);

The Scanner class offers a number of methods to get inputs, and some of them are "nextInt," "nextLong," "nextFloat," "nextDouble," "nextLine," "next," "hasNextInt," "hasNextDouble" and "close." We will be using the next method to collect text inputs and the nextDouble method to collect numbers. The hasNext method series help us ensure that the next value is going to be of that specified type. For example, if we want to ensure that the next value entered is an integer, we can check it using hasNextInt method. This method will return true only if the next value entered is an integer.

In this section, we have seen how to use the Scanner class to collect both text and number inputs from the user.

Talking Calculator Development

Yes, we are heading into the actual development of our
Talking Calculator. By the end of this section, you will have a
running calculator ready.

Shall we start? If you have not understood any of the
concepts explained above, please go through it until you get
them clearly because we are going to use all of those concepts
during the development of our Talking Calculator. We plan
to create a calculator that performs the basic mathematic
calculations including addition, subtraction, multiplication,
and division. We also allow the user to interact with the
calculator and have some fun.

Let me tell you one thing before we start. I am not including
comments with each code snippet. However, you should
comment the code yourself as it helps to make sure that you
understand your own code, as well as helping others to
understand your code, and your future self to understand it.
Because as you continue to learn to code, you will come up
with new and different ways to solve programming problems
and, you might not remember your old ways of solving those
problems.

Getting Started

First create a class named "TalkingCalculator." It should be
public as we want to make it accessible to all other classes.

```
public class TalkingCalculator

{
```

```
public static void main(String[] args)

    {



    }

}
```

We will be getting inputs from the user continuously, so we can create a variable to store the input from the user temporarily until we use it or save into appropriate variables. Add the following line of code just after the opening curly brace of the class, before the main method:

```
String userInput;
```

Why did we add it inside the class and not within the main method? Do you remember the variable scope concept we discussed in the Variables section? We need to access this value throughout our program. It should have scope within the whole class. In other words, the scope of the variable should not be limited within any method.

Asking the User's Name

A person always wants to be unique. What makes you unique? Of course, it is your name. That is why you love to be addressed using your name or nickname as opposed to "hey," "kiddo," or "you with the face." Let's also address our user by his or her name. For this, let's ask the name of the user first and store it in a variable so that we can address the user as and when required.

Add the following line of code just next to the statement String userInput.

> *String userName;*

We also need the Scanner class and an object of the Scanner class to collect inputs. So add the following line of code as the first line of your program.

> *import java.util.Scanner;*

After the two variable declarations, add the following line of code.

> *Scanner myScanner = new Scanner(System.in);*

Now your code should look like this:

import java.util.Scanner;

public class TalkingCalculator

{

  String userInput;

  String userName;

  Scanner myScanner = new Scanner(System.in);

  public static void main(String[] args)

```
    {



    }

    }
```

Next, let's ask the name of the user. Then, let's ask him whether he wants to do mathematical calculations or just talk with the calculator. Based on the user's choice, we will further proceed. Shall we try to implement this part using a method? It will help us organize our code better. Our calculator starts with this method. So, let's name the method "start." We are going to make it an instance method which does not return anything in specific. So, add the following lines of code within the TalkingCalculator class after the main method.

```
    public void start()

    {



    }
```

Let's ask the user his or her name with this:

```
System.out.println("Hello, What is your name?");
```

Let's temporarily get it inside the userInput variable and then pass it to the userName variable. In fact, this time you can directly collect the input, that is the user name, in the variable userName itself instead of collecting it first in userInput variable and then storing in the userName variable. However, when we collect other inputs, we will get it in userInput variable. Just to maintain uniformity, we collect the user name as well in userInput variable and then pass it to userName variable. Add the following lines of code just below the statement that asked for the user name.

userInput = myScanner.next();

userName = userInput;

Next, let's tell the user that his name is really cool just to make him happy. Add the following line of code.

System.out.println(userName + ". That's a cool name!!!");

Setting up the System to Either Talk or Do Math

Now we are into our serious business, we are going to ask whether he wants math or talk. If he answers math, we will allow him to do mathematic operations, and if he answers talk, we will allow him to have some fun. If he does not answer math or talk, we will tell the user that we did not get the correct answer. So, first ask the user.

System.out.println("Do you want to do some math? or just talk?");

userInput = myScanner.next();

Next, based on the input, we allow the user to proceed accordingly calling different methods. So here we have to use conditional statements which we have discussed already.

```
if(userInput.equalsIgnoreCase("math"))

    {

            calculate();

    }

else if(userInput.equalsIgnoreCase("talk"))

    {

            talk();

    }

else

    {

            System.out.println("Hey " + userName + ". Why
are you not answering me correctly? " + userInput + " doesn't answer
my question!");

            whatNext();

    }
```

We used the equalsIgnoreCase method to perform a "case-insensitive" comparison. What is meant by case-insensitive?

A case-insensitive comparison means we compare the content regardless of its case (upper-case or lower-case). For example, if we compare two strings, "JOHN" and "John", a case sensitive comparison will tell us that they are not the same, whereas a case insensitive comparison will tell that they are the same. Here, let's be somewhat lenient. We will allow the user to do math whether he enters Math or MATH, and we'll us the same with talk.

Now we have just created the start method, but have not invoked it. Where should we call this method? It should be called inside the main method. As we declared the method as non-static, first create an object of the class TalkingCalculator, and then call the method like this.

TalkingCalculator calculator = new TalkingCalculator();

calculator.start();

Next, we need to do math or talk based on what the user wants. Once the math or talk operation is over, we can ask the user what he wants to do next.

So, let's create the methods calculate(), talk() and whatNext() one by one.

Programming the Math Section

Let's start with calculate() method. What is the purpose of calculate method? It should first ask the user what he wants to do, like addition, subtraction, multiplication, or division. Make sure that the program does not die even if he does not answer correctly. If he enters the operation he wants to perform, let's collect two numbers from the user and perform the operation. Do not forget to check whether the user enters number or not.

First, let's create two variables to store the two numbers for the mathematical operation. We do not know whether the user will enter integers or decimal values. To be on the safe side, let's create the variables of double data type.

```
double firstNum;

double secondNum;
```

Next let's ask the user what he wants to do and then collect that input.

```
System.out.println("Do you want to add, subtract, multiply, or divide?");

userInput = myScanner.next();
```

Next we need to check whether the user enters any of the above four options. What if the user enters + instead of add? Not only can we ot process the input, but also the program might die. To avoid this, make sure that he enters one of the above four options and warn him if he does not.

```
if(!userInput.equalsIgnoreCase("add") &&
!userInput.equalsIgnoreCase("subtract")
```

&&!userInput.equalsIgnoreCase("multiply")&&
userInput.equalsIgnoreCase("divide"))

> {
>
>> *System.out.println(userInput + " doesn't answer my question. Be careful " + userName);*
>
>> *calculate();*
>
> }

Don't get tense by seeing the lengthy condition. The && logical operator is used here to check whether all these conditions are satisfied or not. It means to check whether this is true AND this is true. If only one of the two things is true, then it returns false.

!userInput.equalsIgnoreCase("add") means user enters something other than add. The ! logical operator means "not", so if the user enters something that does not equal "add," then it will return true. The fact that all the four conditions (between &&) are satisfied means that the user has entered something other than add, subtract, multiply, and divide. Then we will ask the user to enter a correct value. We are calling the calculate method to ask again what he wants to do.

Otherwise, we are collecting two numbers from the user and making sure that he enters numbers, not strings. We use the hasNextDouble method to make sure that the number entered is of type double. If the user does not enter a double value, we tell them that they messed up and entered something else. In that case, we call the calculate method again so that the user will be asked again what he wants to do.

```
        System.out.println("what do you want to " + userInput +
"?");

        System.out.print("First Number: ");


        if(myScanner.hasNextDouble())

        {

                firstNum = myScanner.nextDouble();

        }

        else

        {

                System.out.println(userName + " do you not like me? If
I didn't catch that it could have killed me!" + myScanner.next() + " is
not a number!");

                calculate();

        }


        System.out.println("\nGreat!");

        System.out.print("Now for the Second Number: ");


        if(myScanner.hasNextDouble())

        {
```

```
            secondNum = myScanner.nextDouble();

    }

    else

    {

            System.out.println(userName + " do you not like me? If
I didn't catch that it could have killed me! " + myScanner.next() + " is
not a number!");

            calculate();

    }



    System.out.println("\n");
```

The "\n" inside the System.out.println(); simply means to go down another line. The "ln" on the end of println tells the program that as soon as it is finished outputting, then the next output should go on the next line down. The line of code "System.out.println("\n"); is pretty much telling the program that the next output should be two lines down, instead of just one.

Now we are ready with the operands. Let's do the math based on user's choice.

```
    if(userInput.equalsIgnoreCase("add"))

    {

            System.out.println("Here is your answer: " + (firstNum
+ secondNum));
```

```
    }

    else if(userInput.equalsIgnoreCase("subtract"))

    {

        System.out.println("Here is your answer: " + (firstNum
- secondNum));

    }

    else if(userInput.equalsIgnoreCase("multiply"))

    {

        System.out.println("Here is your answer: " + (firstNum
* secondNum));

    }

    else if(userInput.equalsIgnoreCase("divide"))

    {

        System.out.println("Here is your answer: " + (firstNum
/ secondNum));

    }
```

We finally call the whatNext method to ask the user again what he wants to do next, math or talk.

```
    whatNext();
```

Now your calculate method will look like this:

```
public void calculate()

    {

        double firstNum = 0;

        double secondNum = 0;



        System.out.println("Do you want to add, subtract, multiply,
or divide?");

        userInput = myScanner.next();



        if(!userInput.equalsIgnoreCase("add") &&
!userInput.equalsIgnoreCase("subtract")
&&!userInput.equalsIgnoreCase("multiply")&&
userInput.equalsIgnoreCase("divide"))

            {

                System.out.println(userInput + " doesn't answer my
question. Be careful " + userName);

                calculate();

            }



        System.out.println("what do you want to " + userInput +
"?");
```

```
System.out.print("First Number: ");


if(myScanner.hasNextDouble())

{

    firstNum = myScanner.nextDouble();

}

else

{

        System.out.println(userName + " do you not like me? If
I didn't catch that it could have killed me! " + myScanner.next() + " is
not a number!");

        calculate();

}


System.out.println("\nGreat!");

System.out.print("Now for the Second Number: ");


if(myScanner.hasNextDouble())

{

    secondNum = myScanner.nextDouble();
```

```
        }

    else

    {

            System.out.println(userName + " do you not like me? If
I didn't catch that it could have killed me! " + myScanner.next() + " is
not a number!");

            calculate();

    }

    System.out.println("\n");



    if(userInput.equalsIgnoreCase("add"))

    {

            System.out.println("Here is your answer: " + (firstNum
+ secondNum));

    }

    else if(userInput.equalsIgnoreCase("subtract"))

    {

            System.out.println("Here is your answer: " + (firstNum
- secondNum));

    }

    else if(userInput.equalsIgnoreCase("multiply"))
```

```
        {

                System.out.println("Here is your answer: " + (firstNum
* secondNum));

        }

        else if(userInput.equalsIgnoreCase("divide"))

        {

                System.out.println("Here is your answer: " + (firstNum
/ secondNum));

        }

        whatNext();

        }
```

Programming the Conversation Section

Next we are going to deal with the talk method. In this method, let's try to be friendlier with the user. Let's ask the user his favorite color and animal. Let's answer differently based on his inputs.

We can also have a mind reading game. We will ask the user to find the number that the calculator is thinking of. Suppose we store a number and compare the number entered by the user with the stored number. The user will be able to find out the number the calculator is thinking of just by playing once or twice. Instead, we will use a mathematic technique and create a random number every time so that the number will be different each time. We will use a built-in method Math.random. This method returns a value between 0 and 1.

So, let's multiply it by 10 to get a number between 0 and 10. Sound good?

Here is the talk method.

```
public void talk()
{
    System.out.println("So, what is your favorite color?");
    userInput = myScanner.next();


    if(userInput.equalsIgnoreCase("blue"))
        {
        System.out.println("Really? Cool! me too!");
        }
            else
            {
        System.out.println(userInput + "? My favorite color is
better! I like blue!");
            }


    System.out.println("What is your favorite animal?");
    userInput = myScanner.next();
```

```java
if(userInput.equalsIgnoreCase("wolf"))

        {

    System.out.println("That's cool! me too!");

        }

            else if(userInput.equalsIgnoreCase("dog"))

                {

        System.out.println("Dogs are cool too, they're related to
my favorite animal, the wolf.");

                }

            else if(userInput.equalsIgnoreCase("cat"))

                {

        System.out.println("A cat? Seriously? I like wolves, they
would eat your cat.");

                }

            else

                {

        System.out.println(userInput + " are cool too, but I prefer
wolves.");

                }

        long guess = 0;
```

```java
int randomNumber = (int)(Math.random()*10);


    System.out.println("I have a number between 0 and 10 in
my mind. Can you find it out? If you enter anything that isn't a number
I will die!");


    if(myScanner.hasNextDouble())

        {

    guess = (long) myScanner.nextDouble();


    if(guess == randomNumber)

        {

    System.out.println("That's correct!");

}
        else

        {

        System.out.println("Sorry, that's not it, maybe try
again some other time.");

        System.out.println("The number I was thinking of was
" + randomNumber);

        }
```

```
        }

    else

        {

        System.out.println("You tried to kill me! That wasn't a
number!");

            myScanner.next();

        }

        whatNext();

    }
```

I think now you are at the stage where you can understand this code. Isn't it self-explanatory? Try to understand each line of code on your own.

Writing What's Next

Finally, we are going to write the whatNext method. It's nothing more than the repetition of a part of code in the start method. It asks the user at the end of math or talk operation how he wants to proceed. That is, whether he wants to again do math, just talk, or even close the application. If he wants to close the application, we use the System.exit function to exit the application. Here is the whatNext method.

```
    public void whatNext()

        {
```

```java
        System.out.println("\n\nWhat do you want to do? math?
or talk? or exit?");

        userInput = myScanner.next();



        if(userInput.equalsIgnoreCase("math"))

        {

            calculate();

         }

        else if(userInput.equalsIgnoreCase("talk"))

        {

            talk();

         }

        else if(userInput.equalsIgnoreCase("exit"))

        {

            System.exit(1);

         }

        else

        {

            System.out.println(userName + "!!!! Why are you trying
to confuse me??? " + userInput + " is not a choice!");
```

```
        whatNext();

    }

}
```

Complete Source Code for the Calculator

Since I've explained the code in bits and pieces throughout the text, I am putting the full code below so you have it all in one place for your reference.

```java
import java.util.Scanner;

public class TalkingCalculator
{
    String userInput;

    String userName;

    Scanner myScanner = new Scanner(System.in);

    public static void main(String[] args)
    {
        TalkingCalculator calculator = new TalkingCalculator();

        calculator.start();
    }


    public void start()
    {
        System.out.println("Hello, What is your name?");
```

```java
userInput = myScanner.next();

userName = userInput;

System.out.println(userName + ". That's a cool
name!!!");

System.out.println("Do you want to do some math? or
just talk?");

userInput = myScanner.next();

if(userInput.equalsIgnoreCase("math"))

{

calculate();

}

else if(userInput.equalsIgnoreCase("talk"))

{

talk();

}

else

{

System.out.println("Hey " + userName + ". Why are
you not answering me correctly? " + userInput + " doesn't answer my
question!");

whatNext();
```

```
        }

    }


    public void calculate()

    {

            double firstNum = 0;

        double secondNum = 0;



            System.out.println("Do you want to add, subtract, multiply,
or divide?");

            userInput = myScanner.next();



            if(!userInput.equalsIgnoreCase("add") &&
!userInput.equalsIgnoreCase("subtract") &&

            !userInput.equalsIgnoreCase("multiply") &&
!userInput.equalsIgnoreCase("divide"))

                {

            System.out.println(userInput + " doesn't answer my
question. Be careful " + userName);

            calculate();

        }
```

```java
System.out.println("What do you want to " + userInput + "?");

System.out.print("First Number: ");



if(myScanner.hasNextDouble())

    {

    firstNum = myScanner.nextDouble();

}

        else

        {

    System.out.println(userName + ", do you not like me? If I didn't catch that it could have killed me!" + myScanner.next() + " is not a number!");

            calculate();

}



System.out.println("\nGreat!");

System.out.print("Now for the Second Number: ");



if(myScanner.hasNextDouble())
```

```
        {

        secondNum = myScanner.nextDouble();

    }

        else

        {

        System.out.println(userName + ", do you not like me? If
I didn't catch that it could have killed me!" + myScanner.next() + " is
not a number!");

            calculate();

    }


    System.out.println("\n");


    if(userInput.equalsIgnoreCase("add"))
        {

        System.out.println("Here is your answer: " + (firstNum
+ secondNum));

    }

        else if(userInput.equalsIgnoreCase("subtract"))
        {
```

```java
        System.out.println("Here is your answer: " + (firstNum
- secondNum));

        }

            else if(userInput.equalsIgnoreCase("multiply"))

            {

        System.out.println("Here is your answer: " + (firstNum
* secondNum));

        }

            else if(userInput.equalsIgnoreCase("divide"))

            {

        System.out.println("Here is your answer: " + (firstNum
/ secondNum));

        }

    whatNext();

    }


    public void talk()

    {

    System.out.println("So, what is your favorite color?");

    userInput = myScanner.next();
```

```
if(userInput.equalsIgnoreCase("blue"))

        {

    System.out.println("Really? Cool! me too!");

    }

        else

        {

        System.out.println(userInput + "? My favorite color is
better! I like blue!");

    }



    System.out.println("What is your favorite animal?");

    userInput = myScanner.next();



    if(userInput.equalsIgnoreCase("wolf"))

        {

    System.out.println("That's cool! me too!");

    }

        else if(userInput.equalsIgnoreCase("dog"))

        {
```

```java
        System.out.println("Dogs are cool too, they're related to
my favorite animal, the wolf.");

    }

        else if(userInput.equalsIgnoreCase("cat"))

        {

        System.out.println("A cat? Seriously? I like wolves, they
would eat your cat.");

    }

        else

        {

        System.out.println(userInput + " are cool too, but I prefer
wolves.");

    }

    long guess = 0;

    int randomNumber = (int)(Math.random()*10);


        System.out.println("I have a number between 0 and 10 in
my mind. Can you find it out? If you enter anything that isn't a number
I will die!");


        if(myScanner.hasNextDouble())

        {
```

```
guess = (long) myScanner.nextDouble();


if(guess == randomNumber)

    {

    System.out.println("That's correct!");

    }

        else

        {

    System.out.println("Sorry, that's not it, maybe try
again some other time.");

        System.out.println("The number I was thinking of was
" + randomNumber);

        }

        }

        else

        {

        System.out.println("You tried to kill me! That wasn't a
number!");

        myScanner.next();

    }

    whatNext();
```

```
}


public void whatNext()

{

    System.out.println("\n\nWhat do you want to do? math?
or talk? or exit?");

    userInput = myScanner.next();


    if(userInput.equalsIgnoreCase("math"))

        {

    calculate();

}

        else if(userInput.equalsIgnoreCase("talk"))

            {

    talk();

}

        else if(userInput.equalsIgnoreCase("exit"))

            {

    System.exit(1);

}
```

```
        else

            {

                System.out.println(userName + "!!!! Why are you trying
to confuse me??? " + userInput + " is not a choice!");

                whatNext();

            }

        }

    }
```

Our Talking Calculator is ready now. Compile and execute. You will get the output. In this section, we have applied all our learning to create a cool Talking Calculator.

Conclusion

Now you have learned a number of Java concepts. You have seen how a Java program is processed using java compiler and Java Virtual Machine. You also have set up the basic development environment by installing Notepad++ and JDK. You understand what object oriented programming is. You have also learned about variables, methods, operators, and the Scanner class. Above all, you have developed a cool and wonderful Talking Calculator on your own.

Do you remember that I promised to help you in setting up a complex development environment? With the basic setup we have, we need to go to the command prompt every time to compile and run our Java programs. However, if you want to make the whole process of development and execution a lot easier, you can install any of the popular Integrated Development Environments. If you want to, you can get NetBeans or Eclipse from the Internet and install it. The procedure you need to follow is almost the same. Try it if you want.

You have learned the basics of Java, and the equivalent to a college programming class! Now you are in a position to understand advanced Java material on your own. Try to learn more and develop wonderful Java applications. I wish you luck for all your future Java learning endeavors!!!

Chandler

Made in the USA
Lexington, KY
02 September 2016